Copyright & Disclaimer

Travel Like A Local (Map Book) By Maxwell Fox (2019)

Map Created on Inkatlas.com.

Copyright OpenStreetMap contributors (openstreetmap.org), Inkatlas.

OpenStreetMap data incl. legend/map key is based on CC-BY-SA license.

Travel Planner & Lined Paper Pages by ShastaCrafts.

The information and images contained in this book, for example cover art, is protected under all Federal and International Copyright Laws and Treaties. Therefore, any use or reprint of the material in the book, either paperback or electronic, is prohibited. Users may not transmit or reproduce the material in any way shape or form – mechanically or electronically such as recording, photocopying or information storage and retrieval system – without getting prior written permission from the publisher/author.

All attempts have been made to verify the information contained in this book, but the author and publisher do not bear any responsibility for errors or omissions. Any perceived negative connotation of any individual, group, or company is purely unintentional. Furthermore, this book is intended as entertainment only and as such, any and all responsibility for actions taken by reading this book lies with the reader alone and not with the author or publisher. This book is not intended as medical, legal, or business advice and the reader alone holds sole responsibility for any consequences of any actions taken after reading this book. Additionally, it is the reader's responsibility alone and not the author's or publisher's to ensure that all applicable laws and regulations for the business practice are adhered to.

About Maxwell Fox

With a taste for adventure, Maxwell Fox has always been passionate about one thing: traveling.

Ever since he was a little boy he was filled with a unique curiosity and an adventurous spirit that took him along to beautiful and amazing new experiences. From short trips with family to imaginary travels around the world, his wanderlust was his driving force from a young age.

He was fascinated by the endless possibilities of new lands, people and ways of life and that is exactly what he looked to discover every time he went on a new adventure.

From trying the local cuisine and exploring brand new flavors, to visiting all the important cultural and historical sights, he carefully planned each trip so he could experience each place to the fullest and discover every little corner.

What he was after was not the tourist experience but the unique immersion into a new community and a different culture.

So what he did was strive to experience each city like a true local.

Traveling gave him the opportunity to increase his knowledge and interest in history, culture, art, architecture and language. Through his experiences he sought to improve his skills and become the best version of himself.

After his many adventures and life changing experiences, he tried to find a path that would excite him just as much as traveling did.

So he thought of what travelers everywhere have in common and what thing brings all his interests together. And that's how he started his journey through the artful science of cartography.

With a formal training in cartography and a unique love for traveling and adventure, Maxwell Fox decided to make it his life's mission to help fellow travelers around the world have the most amazing experience every time they travel.

ACCOMMODATION

 Hotel

 Motel

 Hostel

 Camping

FOOD & DRINK

 Restaurant

 Fast food

 Cafe

 Ice cream

 Bar

 Pub

SHOP & SERVICE

 Supermarket

 Depertment store

 Marketplace

 Kiosk

 Greengrocer

 Alcohol

 Confectionery

 Bakery

 Tea

Electronics

Computer

Mobile

Hifi

Clothes

Shoes

 Jewellery

 Bag

 Beauty

 Perfumery

 Hairdresser

 Laundry

 Travel agency

 Books

 Art

 Gift

 Toys

 Florist

TRANSPORTATION

 Parking

 Taxi

 Bus stop

 Bus station

 Subway entrance

 Rental car

 Fuel

 Charging station

 Rental bicycle

 Aerodrome

 Helipad

Ferry

ENTERTAINMENT, ARTS & CULTURE

 Cinema

 Theatre

Nightclub

Museum

Library

Artwork

Arts Center

Fountain

Viewpoint

FINANCIAL

Atm

Bank

ACTIVITY

Fitness

Swimming

Golf

Miniature golf

Playground

HEALTHCARE

Hospital

Doctor

Pharmacy

Dentist

Optician

POST

Post box

Post office

LAND USE

Highway

Primary road

Secondary road

Tertiary road

Unclassifield road

Railway

Tram railway

Ferry road

Water

Beach

Volcano

Border

Quarry

Comemercial

Nature

Park

Residential area

OTHER

Information

Toilets

Waste basket

Drinking water

Table

Bench

Elevator

Police

Fire station

Courthouse

Embassy

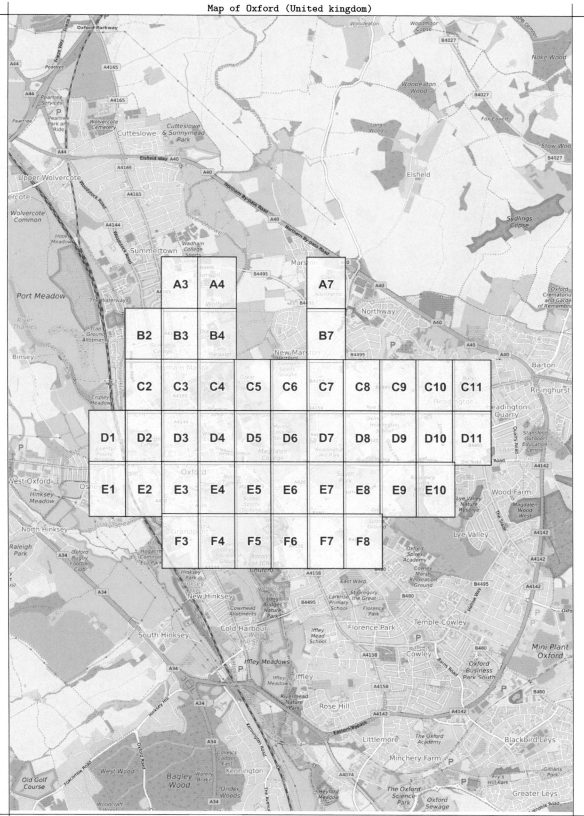

This is an inkatlas. Create your own at inkatlas.com!

1

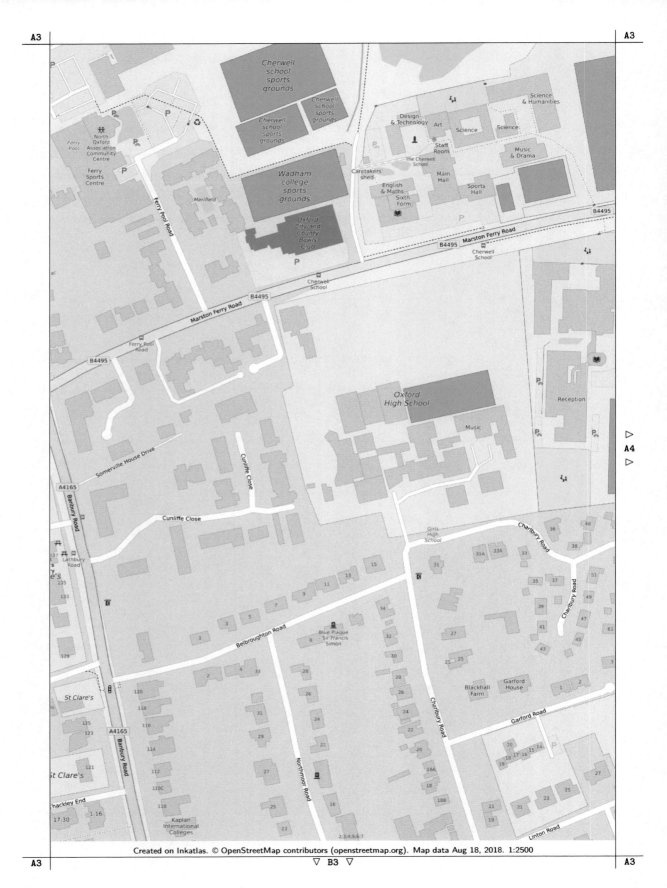

B4495

Marston Ferry Road

B4495

Marston Ferry Road

B4495

P

Oxford
Harlequins

Cherwell
School

P

P

46

42   44

48

50

52   54

Charlbury Road

53

55

51

57

71

59

49

69

61   63   65   67

Catherine
Marriott
Building

Squash
Court

Robin
Gandy
North

M block

River Cherwell or Hinksey

Robin
Gandy
South

E Block

F Block

G Block

H Block

3

4

5

31

Tree Quad

D Block

C Block

27

Whitley
V aircraft
crash
memorial
plaque

P

Wolfson
Harbour

Wolfson
College

North
Mead

Annexe

Berlin
Quad

A Block

River Quad

P

B Block

River Cherwell

Created on Inkatlas. © OpenStreetMap contributors (openstreetmap.org). Map data Aug 18, 2018. 1:2500

▽ B4 ▽

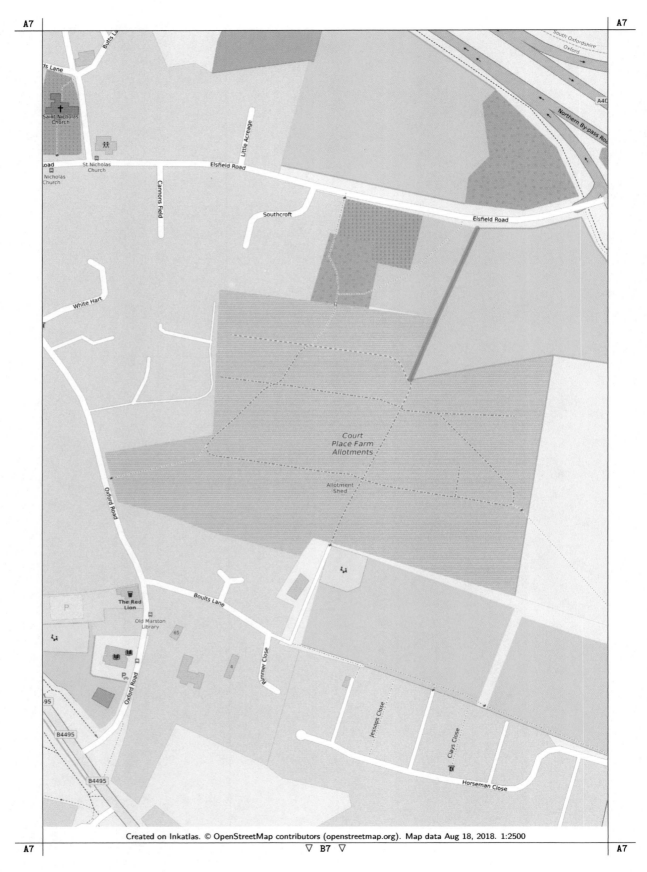

Butts Lane

ds Lane

Saint Nicholas Church

Road

Nicholas Church

St Nicholas Church

Little Acreage

Elsfield Road

South Oxfordshire
Oxford

A40

Northern By-pass Road

Elsfield Road

Cannons Field

Southcroft

White Hart

Court Place Farm Allotments

Allotment Shed

Oxford Road

The Red Lion

P

Old Marston Library

65

Boults Lane

P

Rimmer Close

95

B4495

B4495

Jessops Close

Clays Close

Horseman Close

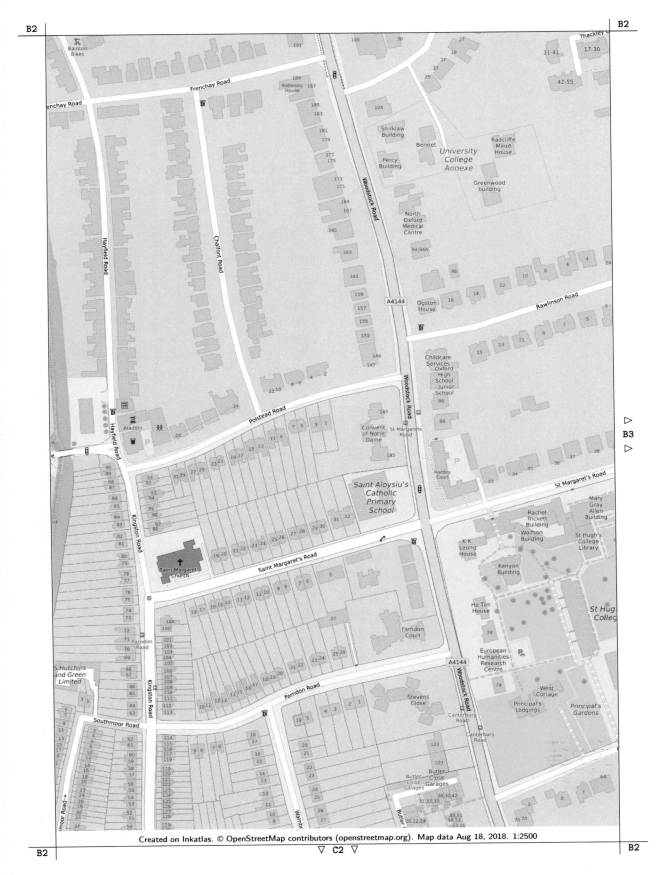

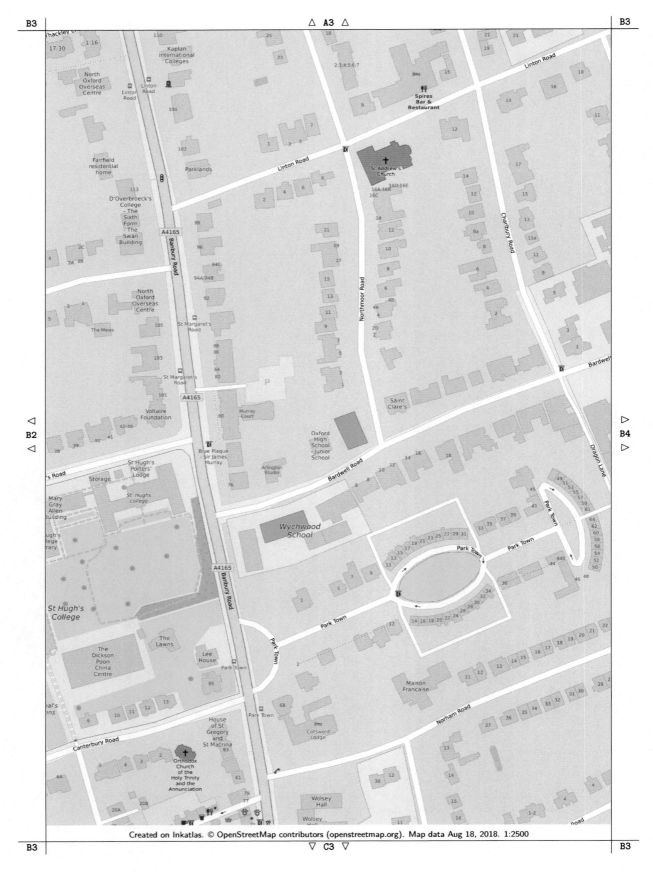

Created on Inkatlas. © OpenStreetMap contributors (openstreetmap.org). Map data Aug 18, 2018. 1:2500

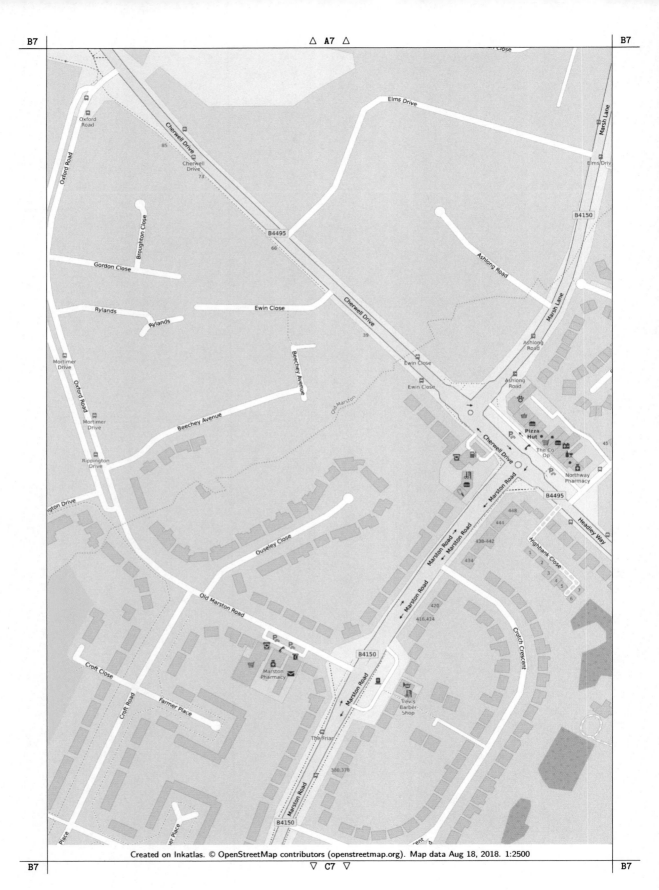

Southmoor Road
Tackley Place
Kingston Road
Tackley Place
Southmoor Place
Warnborough Road
Butter Close
Garages

Oxford Centre for Mission Studies
Latin American Centre
A4144 Church Walk
Church
The Vicarage
Middle East Centre
Saltbridge Building
Woodstock Road

Leckford Road
Hart-Synnot House

Leckford Place School

Plantation Road
A4144
Belsyre Garage
Plantation Road
Gate Building

Wyndham House
Ox Flooring
Leckford Place

Longworth Road
The Grog Shop
Kingston Road

Belmont Drinking Fountain
Walton Well Road
Victoria Arms

Saint Bernard's Road
Belsyre Court
Sirene

▷
C3
▷

The Victoria
Kingston Court

Furnace House
Eagle House
Londis
Walton Street Cycles
Casa Rose Boudoir
Copa

Adelaide Street
Observatory Street

Lord Napier House

Squash Courts
Green Templeton College
Observatory House

St Sepulchre's Cemetery

Brasserie Blanc
Mezzeto
Branca
Saint Paul's House

Doll Building
Radcliffe Observatory
Meeting and Reading Rooms
Gibson Building
Rotunda
Harkness Building

Juxon Street
Walton Street

Phoenix Cinema
Mind

Venables Close
Cranham Street
Phoenix Picturehouse

New Radcliffe House
Jericho Health Centre

Radcliffe Observatory Quarter

Walton Street Cycles Workshop
Cranham Terrace
Jude the Obscure
Reside

Juxon House
Alma Street
Blomfield Place
Jericho Street
King Street
Cardigan Street

mount Street
Hart Stre

The Harcourt Arms
St. Barnabas' C.E. School

Freud
Blavatnik School of Government

Somerville College Accommodation Block
Holtby

The Co operative Food
Walton's
Somerville College
Park

Walton

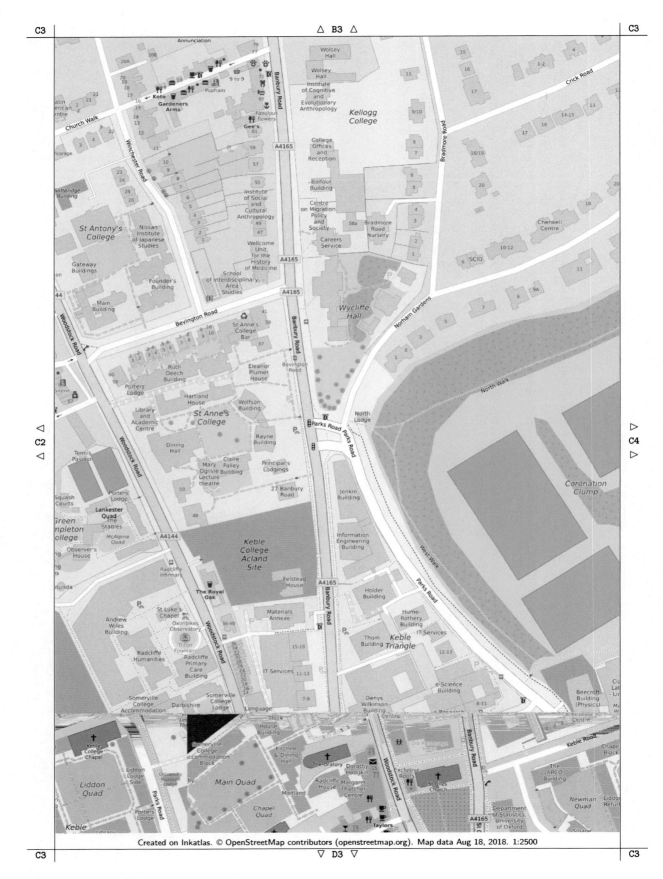

Created on Inkatlas. © OpenStreetMap contributors (openstreetmap.org). Map data Aug 18, 2018. 1:2500

Front Quad
Talbot Hall
Wolfson West
Eleanor Lodge
Donald Fothergill
1
13
14
Porters' Lodge
15
Old Old Hall
New Old Hall
12
Jerome Bruner Building
26
19
22-24
26
Brockhues Lodge
20
Norham Gardens
Department of Education
13A
Department of Education
13

Lazenbee's ... Walk
Lazenbee's Pond
River ...
Old Marston
High Bridge
River ...

North Walk
Oak Walk
North Walk
Thorn Walk
Tentorium

University Parks
Oak Walk

University Cricket Pavillion
Thorn Walk

South Walk
South Walk
South Walk
South Walk

...tion ...np

Henry Wellcome Building of Gene Function
Old Observatory
Medical Sciences Teaching Centre
Dunn School Japanese Garden

Clarendon Laboratory - Lindemann
Sherrington Building
Rodney Porter Building
Oxford Molecular Pathology Institute
Sir William Dunn School of Pathology

...oft ...ing ...cs)
Martin Wood Lecture Theatre
Rex Richards Building
Darlington Link
South Lodge

Clarendon Laboratory - Townsend
Haldane Road
Sherrington Road
Department of Biochemistry
Sherard Road

University Museum Lodge
Blue plaque: Clarendon Laboratory
Atmospheric Physics
Hinshelwood Road
Sibthorp Road
South Parks Road
Department of Psychology

...Road
Robert Hooke Building
Dorothy Hodgkin Road
Le Gros Clark Building
Science Area
Dyson Perrins ...

Created on Inkatlas. © OpenStreetMap contributors (openstreetmap.org). Map data Aug 18, 2018. 1:2500

Little Mill
Pond Mead

Marston Brook

High
Bridge

River Cherwell

Great
Mill Pond
Mead

Old Marston

River Cherwell

Edgeway Road

Oak Walk

River Cherwell

Parson's
Pleasure

Marston Cyclepath

Marston Cyclepath

Marston Cyclepath

Marston Cyclepath

Abraham

Reception   Courtyard

Linacre
College

Bamborough

Mesopotamia Walk

River Cherwell

Music
Meadow

Created on Inkatlas. © OpenStreetMap contributors (openstreetmap.org). Map data Aug 18, 2018. 1:2500

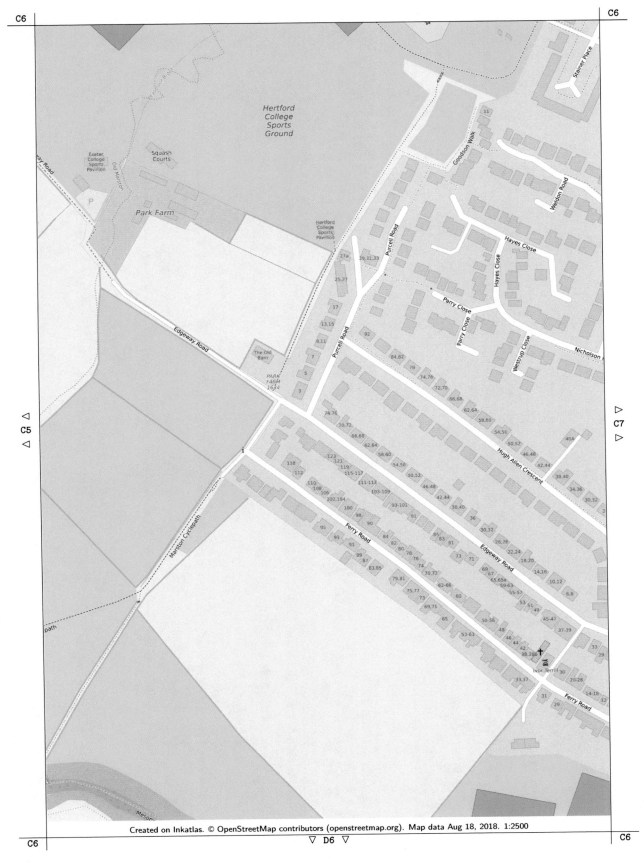

Created on Inkatlas. © OpenStreetMap contributors (openstreetmap.org). Map data Aug 18, 2018. 1:2500

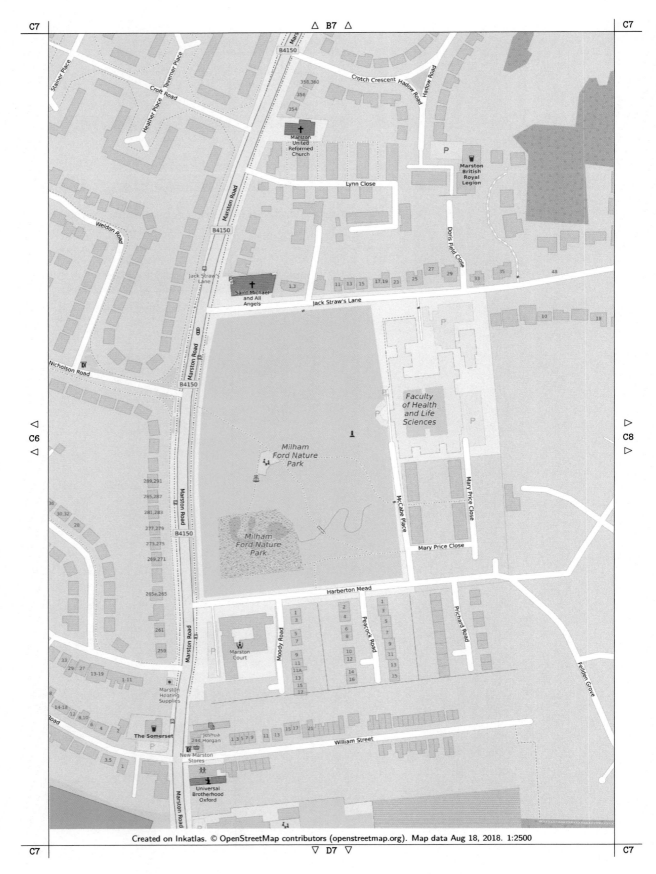

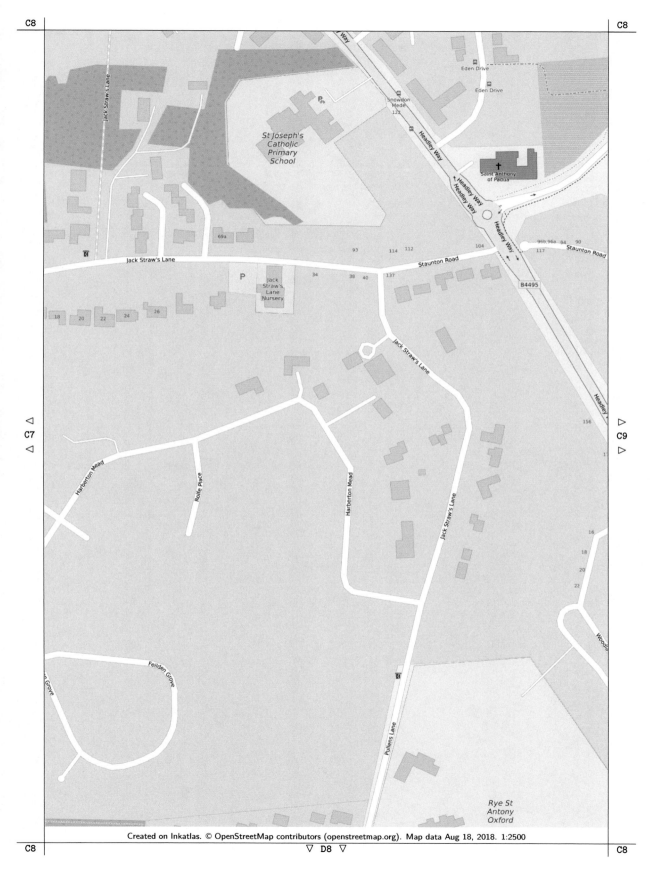

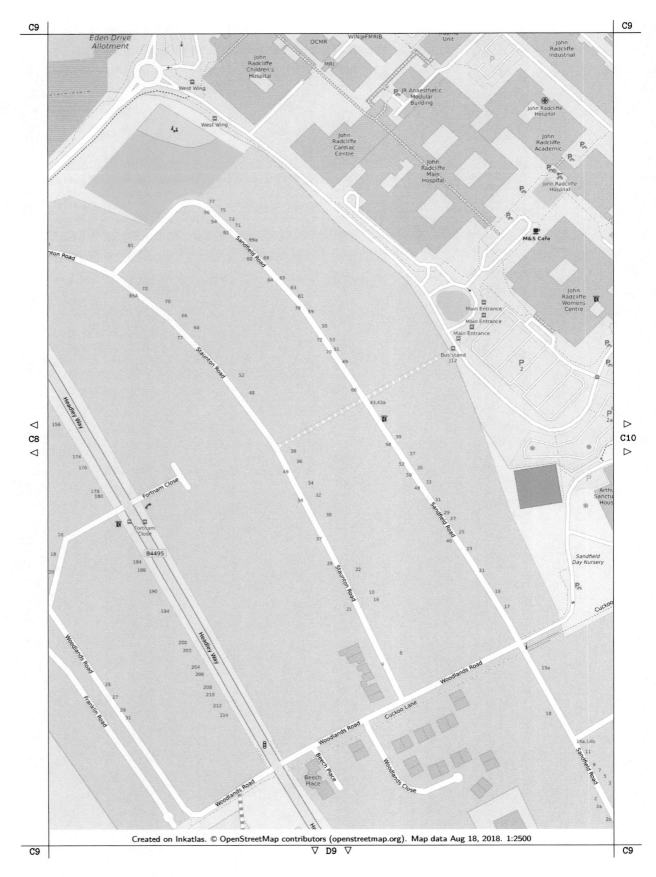

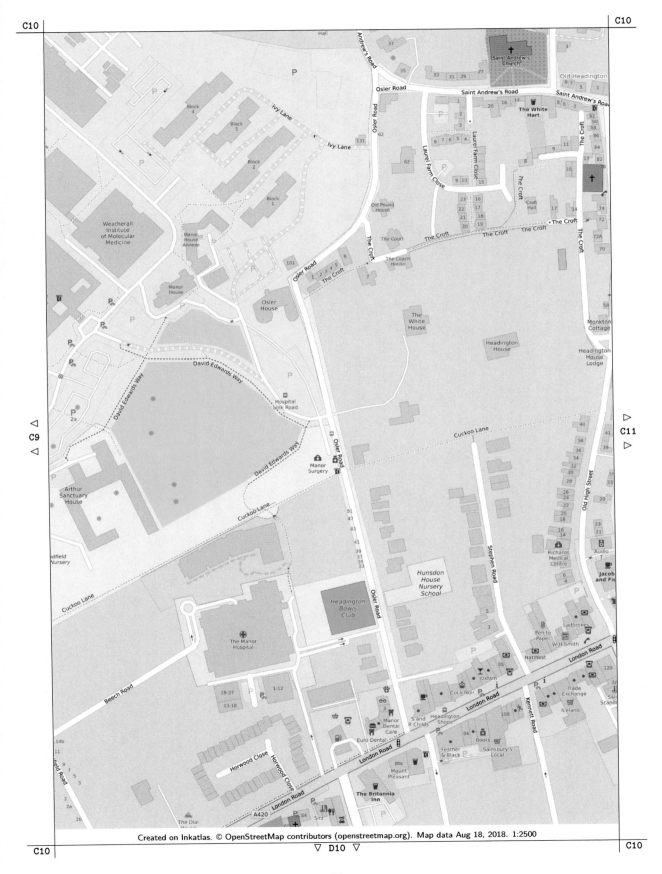

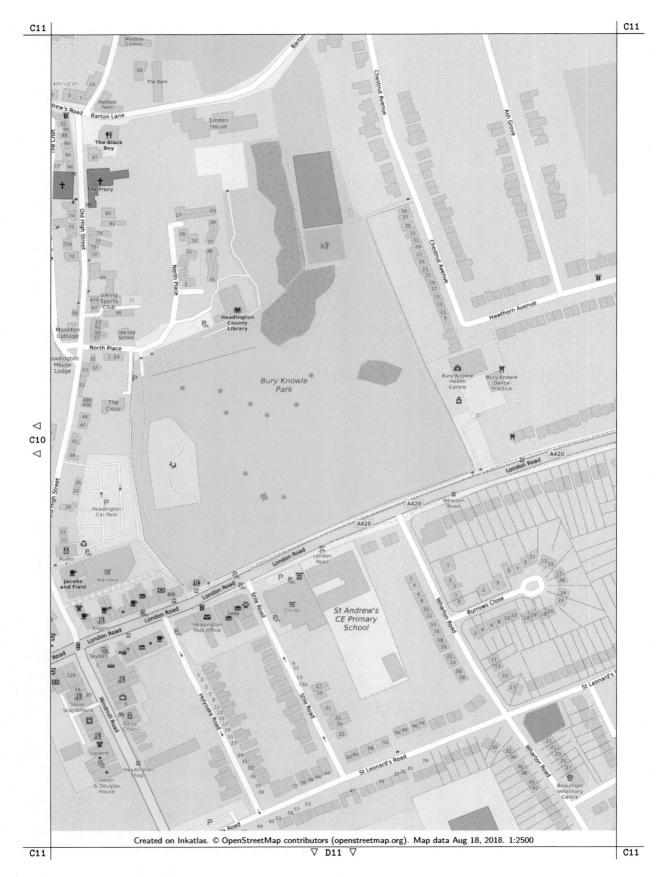

Block
C

Block
B

Block
A

Castle Mill

1-24

Combe Road

Dawson Place

College
Cruisers

St Barna
Church

Chancellor
Park

Venneit Close

P Venneit Close

Roger Dudman Way

Castle Mill Stream

Castle
Mill Boatyard

87

River Thames

River Thames

Roger Dudman Way

Rewley Road

P

P

The
Co-operative
Childcare
Oxford

Rewley
Road
(LMS)
Swing
Bridge

Sheepwash chan

Rewley Road

Tumbling Bulstak Stream
Bay

77
75
73
71
69
67
65
63
61
59
57
55
53
51
49
47
45
43
41
39

P

Oxford

37
35

33
31

28
26

29

29A

27
25

23
21

Abbey Road

19
17

Oxford

Twenty
Pound
Meadow

River Thames

15
13

Roger Dudman Way

11
9

Cripley Road

P

Tra

7
5
3

Cripley Place

P

Radcliffe
House

Wyhtam
House

Pumpkin
Cafe

Oxf
Rail S

Beaumont
Gate

Oxford

O
Rail

Kingerlee
House

The
One
Garage

WHSmith

West Oxford

YHA Oxford

P

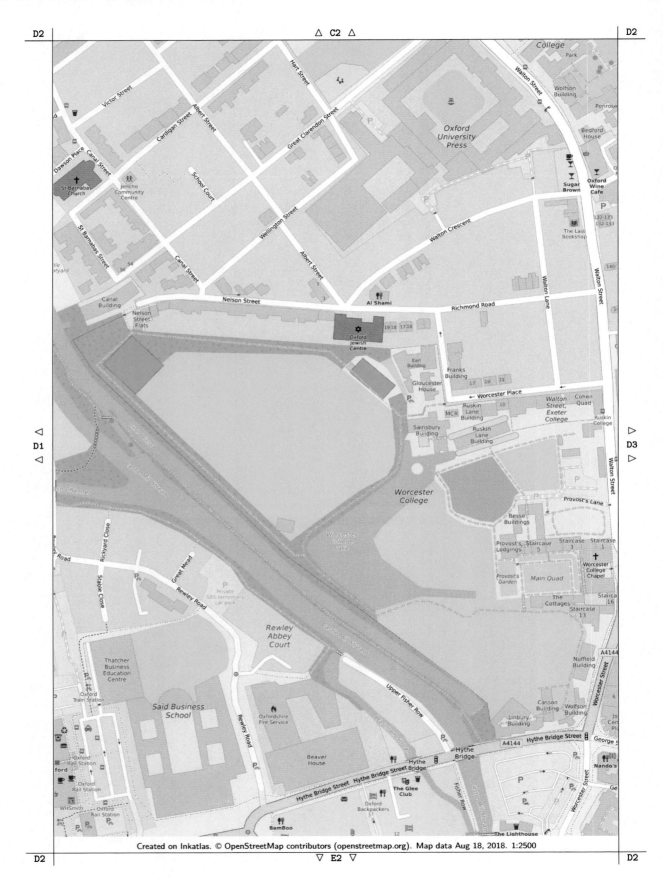

Created on Inkatlas. © OpenStreetMap contributors (openstreetmap.org). Map data Aug 18, 2018. 1:2500

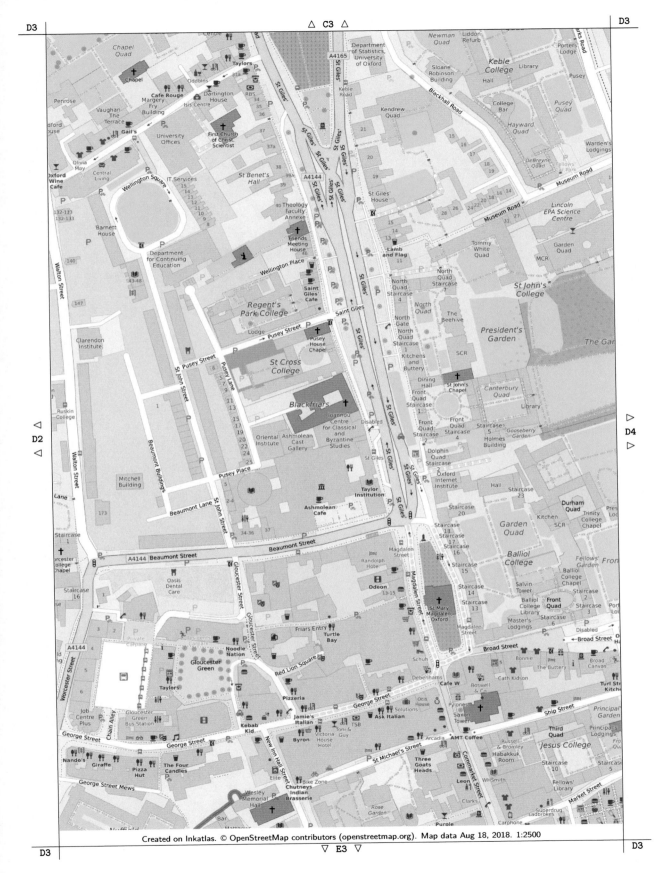

Created on Inkatlas. © OpenStreetMap contributors (openstreetmap.org). Map data Aug 18, 2018. 1:2500

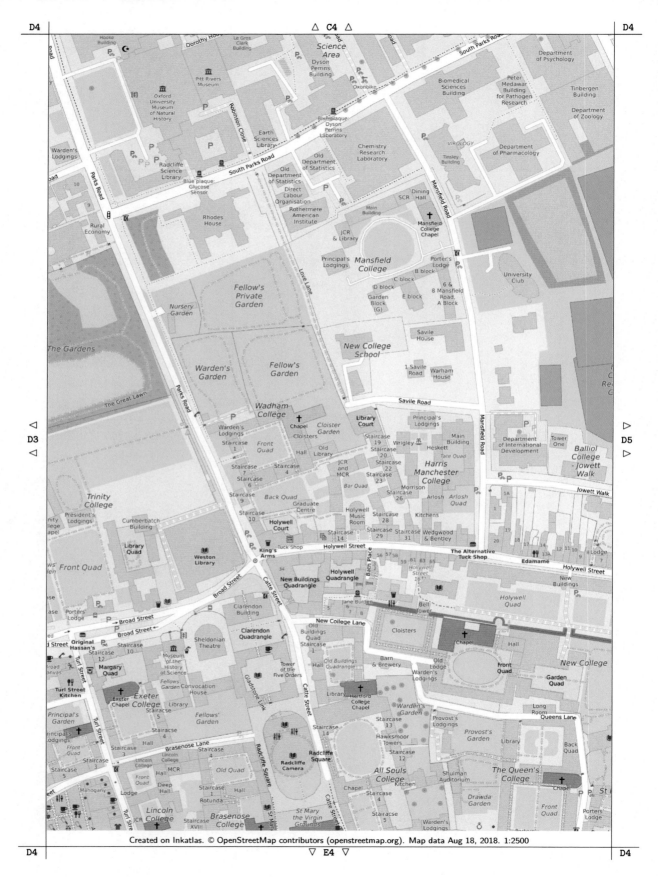

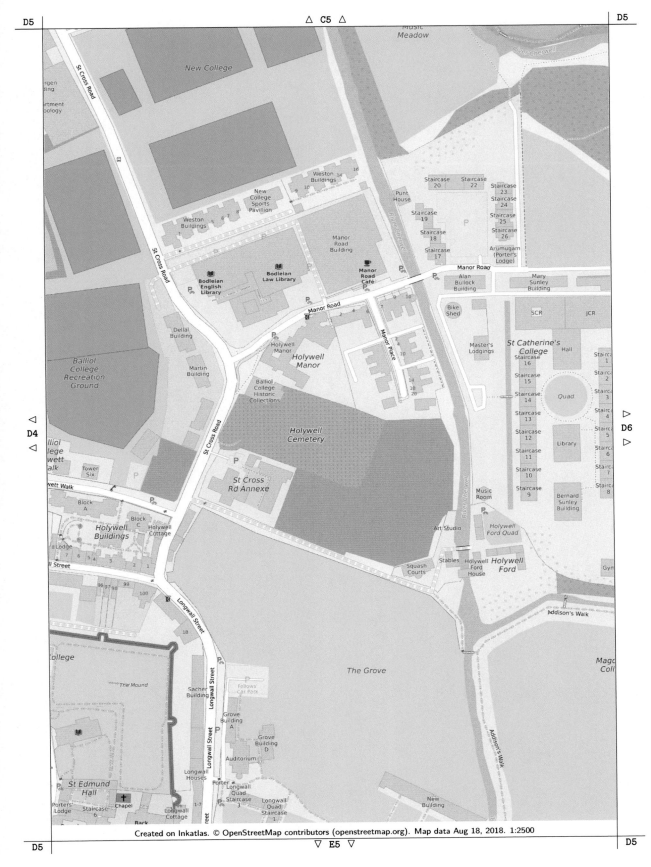

Created on Inkatlas. © OpenStreetMap contributors (openstreetmap.org). Map data Aug 18, 2018. 1:2500

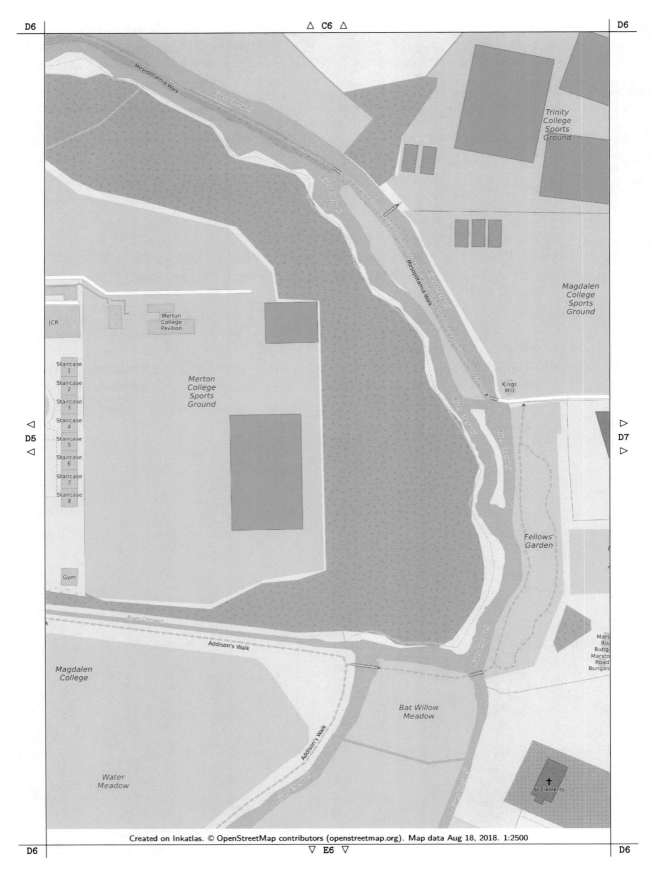

Created on Inkatlas. © OpenStreetMap contributors (openstreetmap.org). Map data Aug 18, 2018. 1:2500

Universal
Brotherhood
Oxford

Marston Road

B4150

John Garne Way

John Garne Way

Clive Booth Hall

Marston Road

Clive Booth
Student
Village

P

P

P

Clive Booth
Hall

dalen
ege
orts
und

P

Marston
Road Car
Park (Temporary)

B4150

P

Kings
Mill Lane

Kings Mill Lane

C·
Oxford
Centre
for Islamic
Studies

Groundkeeper's
storage
yard

P

Red
Oak
Building

Herb
Garden

Magdalen
College
Astro Turf
Pitch

Old HHH
pool now
filled
in but
still visible
from
first floor

HHH Car
Park

Maxwell's
old Helipad
(out of
use)
Ⓗ

Se
Sh

Marston
Road
Bungalow
Marston
Road
Bungalow

Marston
Road
Bungalow

Headington
Hill Park

Marston Road

A420

Gatehouse

B4150

Headington Road

Cheney
Student
Village

Gatehouse

dington Road

ille Court

Rye St
Antony
Oxford

Pullens Field

The Vines

Pullens Lane

Cuckoo Lane

Cuckoo Lane

Cuckoo Lane

Drama
Studio

Art

Pullens Lane

Oxford
Brookes
University
Headington
Road

Headington Road

Oxford
Brookes
University

A420

Buckley

Gypsy
Lane Site

Colonnade

Abercrombie

Media
centre

HHH Car
park

Oxford
Brookes
University
Headington
Hill Site

Helena
Kennedy
Student
Centre

Brookes
University
Car Park

Gatehouse

A420

Oxford
Brookes
University

Headington Hill

Headington Hill

International
Centre

John
Henry
Brookes

Oxford
Brookes
Universit
Gipsy
Lane Site

Sinclai

Service
Sheds

Headington Hill

Birch
house

Headington Road

Mermaid
Fountain

Torige

20

Studental

Oxford
Brookes
University
Centre
for Sport

Sports
Bar

Oxford
Brookes
University
Centre
for Sport

Cheney
School

Cheney
Student
Village

Cheney Lane

Created on Inkatlas. © OpenStreetMap contributors (openstreetmap.org). Map data Aug 18, 2018. 1:2500

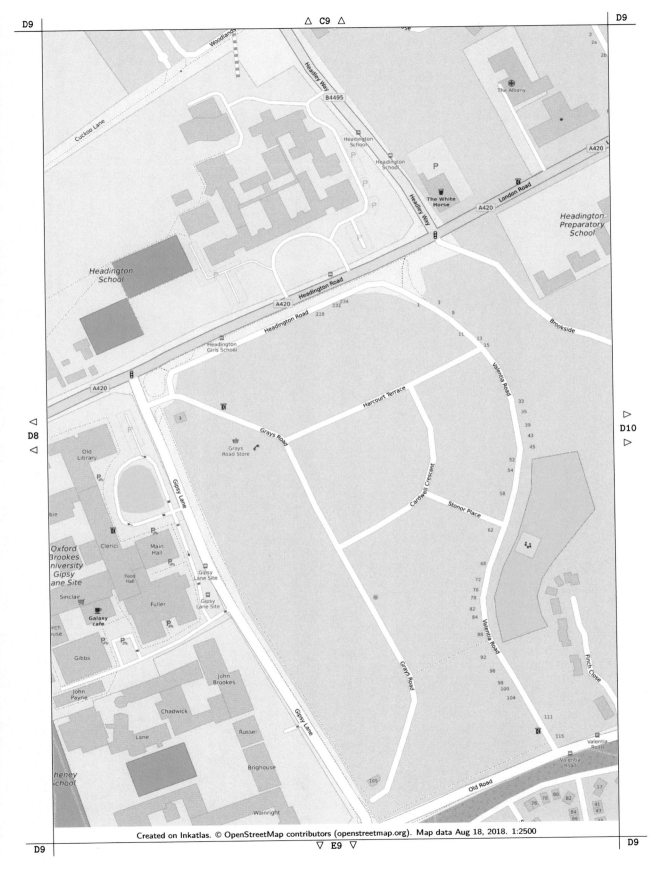

Created on Inkatlas. © OpenStreetMap contributors (openstreetmap.org). Map data Aug 18, 2018. 1:2500

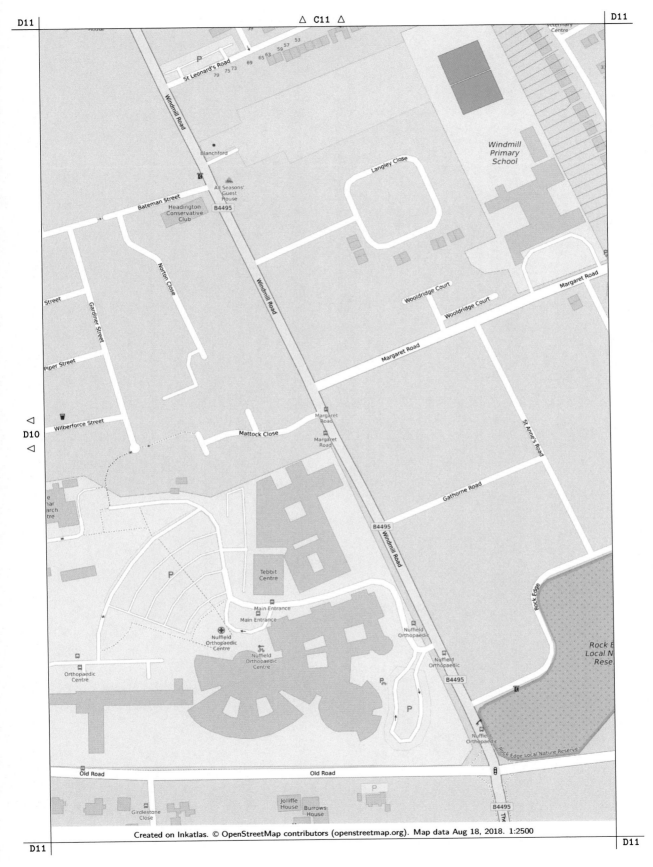

Created on Inkatlas. © OpenStreetMap contributors (openstreetmap.org). Map data Aug 18, 2018. 1:2500

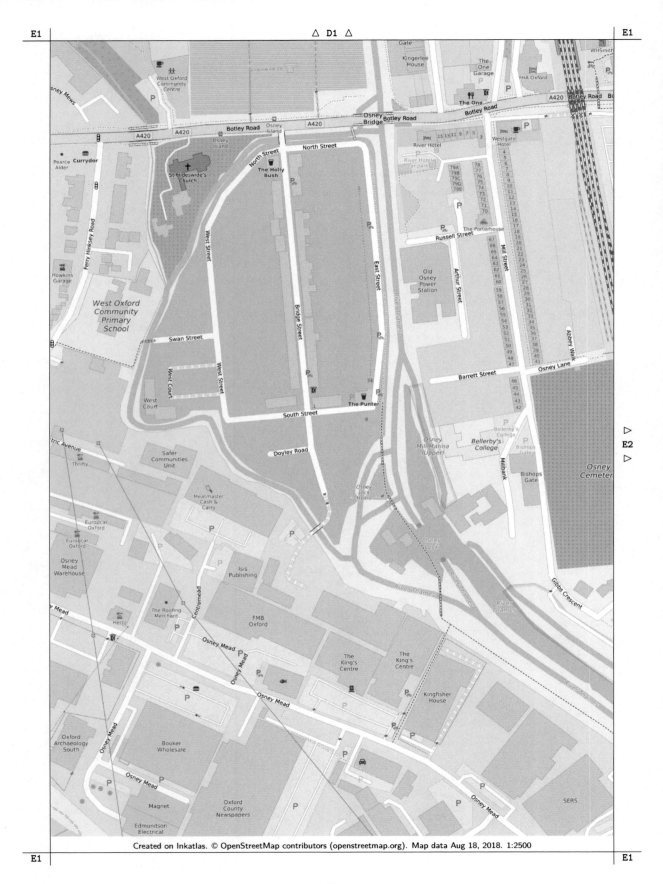

Created on Inkatlas. © OpenStreetMap contributors (openstreetmap.org). Map data Aug 18, 2018. 1:2500

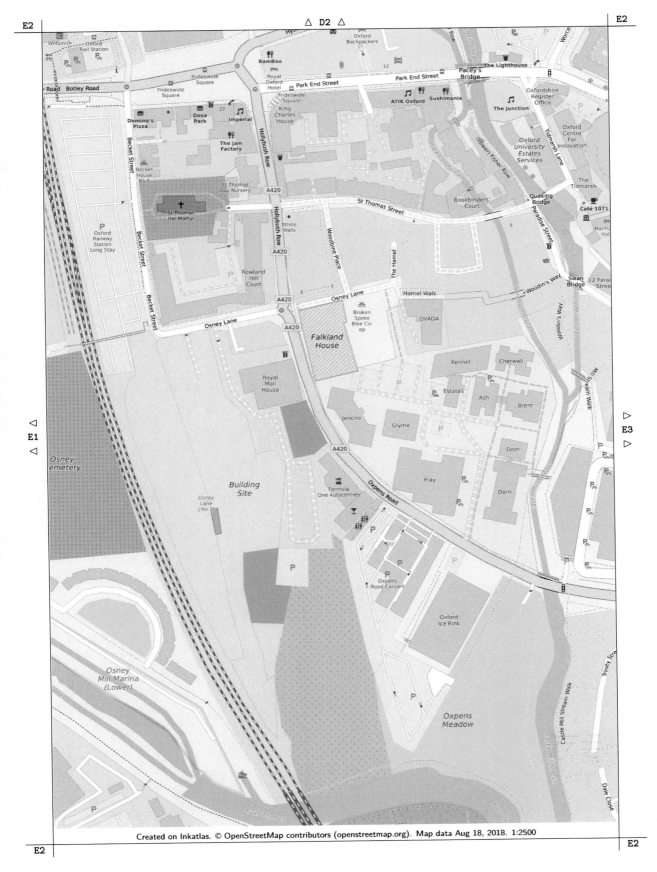

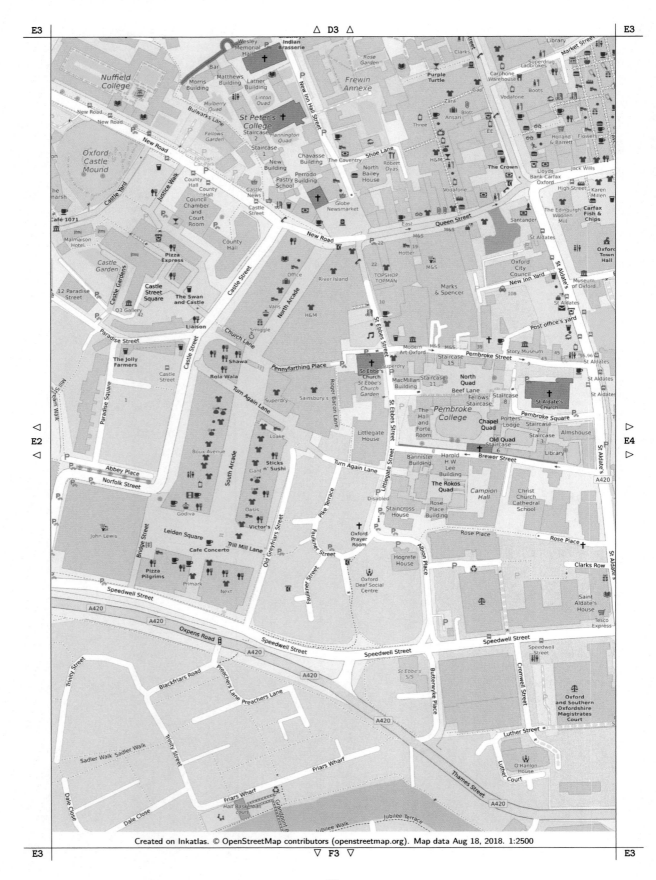

Created on Inkatlas. © OpenStreetMap contributors (openstreetmap.org). Map data Aug 18, 2018. 1:2500

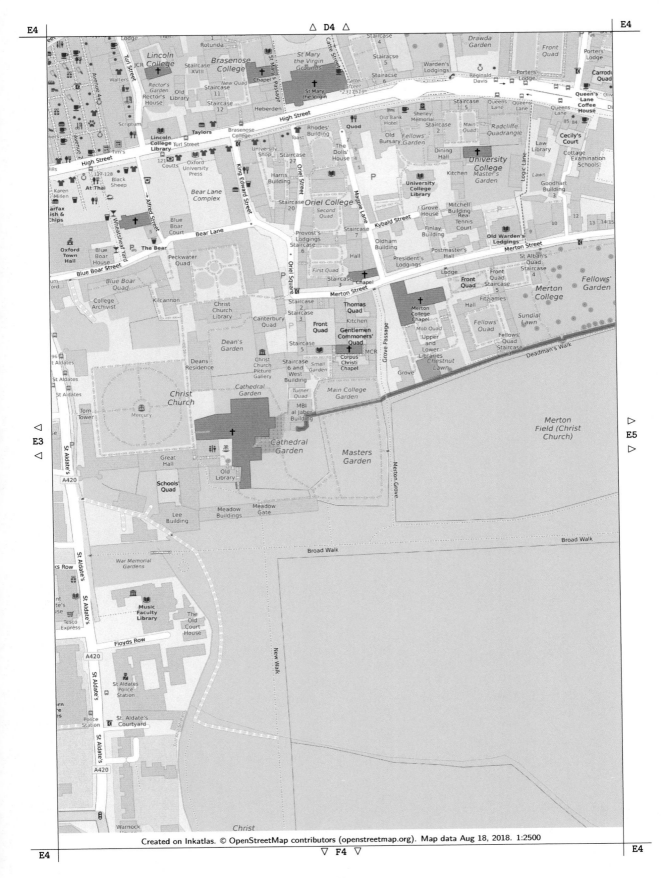

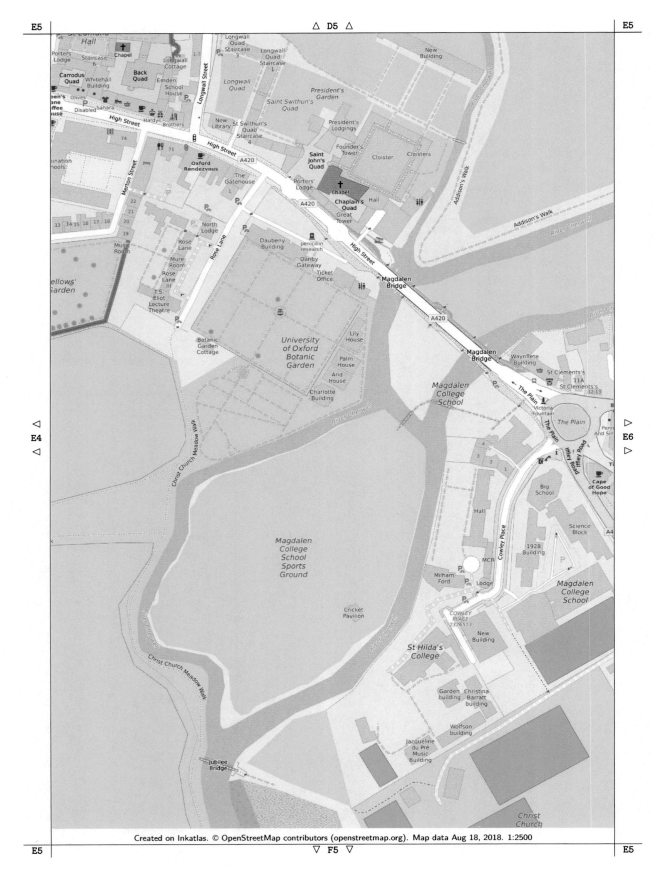

St Edmund Hall

Porters' Lodge

Staircase 6

Chapel

Longwall Cottage

1-7

Longwall Quad Staircase 3

Longwall Quad Staircase 1

New Building

Carrodus Quad

Whitehall Building

Back Quad

Emden School House

Longwall Quad

President's Garden

Olives

Saint Swithun's Quad

President's Lodgings

Disabled

Sahara

High Street

Hardys

Brothers

New Library

St Swithun's Quad Staircase 4

Founder's Tower

Cloister

Cloisters

74

Addison's Walk

Addison's Walk

River Cherwell

71

High Street

A420

Oxford Rendezvous

The Gatehouse

Saint John's Quad

Chapel

Chaplain's Quad

Great Tower

Hall

Porters' Lodge

A420

Merton Street

22

21

20

19

13 14 15 16 17 18

Music Room

North Lodge

Rose Lane

Rose Lane

Daubeny Building

penicillin research

High Street

Magdalen Bridge

Mure Room

Rose Lane III

Danby Gateway

Ticket Office

A420

Magdalen Bridge

Waynflete Building

St Clements's

11A

St Clements's

12-13

T.S. Eliot Lecture Theatre

Fellows' Garden

Botanic Garden Cottage

University of Oxford Botanic Garden

Lily House

Palm House

Arid House

Charlotte Building

The Plain

Magdalen College School

Victoria Fountain

The Plain

E4 ◁ ◁

◁

River Cherwell

4

3

2

1

Peni And Sin

E6 ▷ ▷

Christ Church Meadow Walk

Big School

Cape of Good Hope

Science Block

A4

Cowley Place

Hall

1928 Building

Magdalen College School Sports Ground

MCR

Milham Ford

Lodge

Magdalen College School

River Cherwell

Cricket Pavilion

COWLEY PLACE 2326513

New Building

St Hilda's College

Garden building

Christina Barratt building

Wolfson building

Christ Church Meadow Walk

Jacqueline du Pré Music Building

Jubilee Bridge

Christ Church

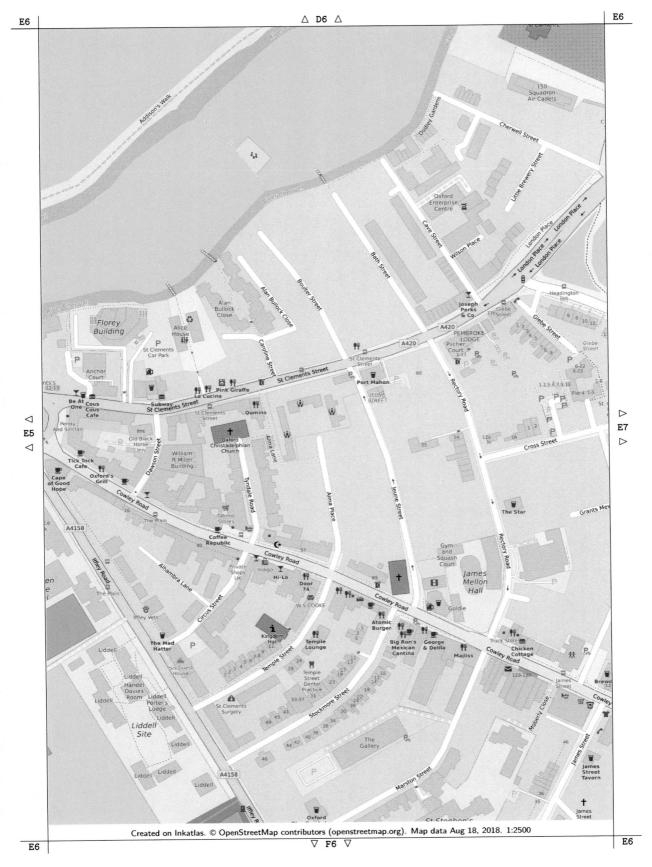

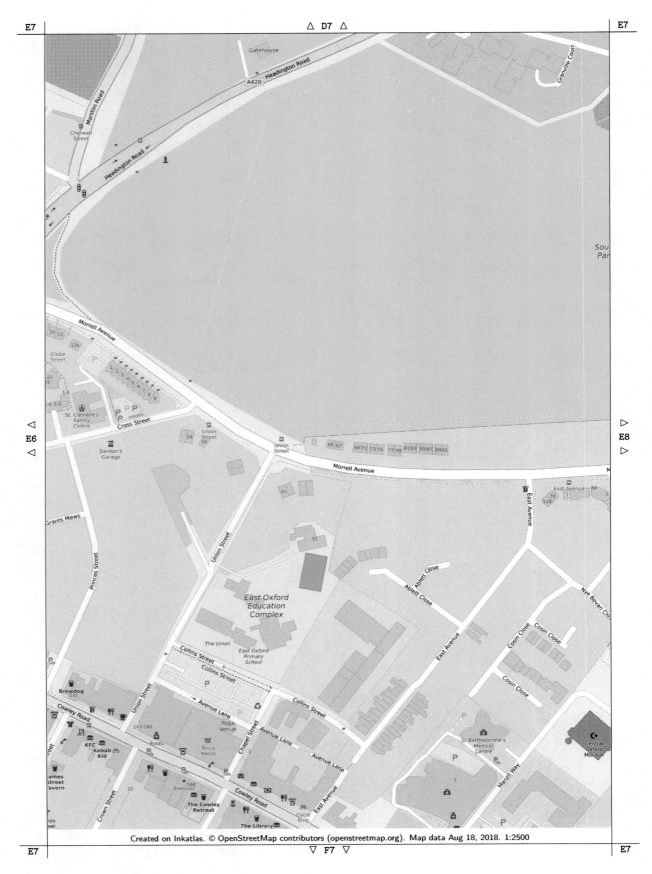

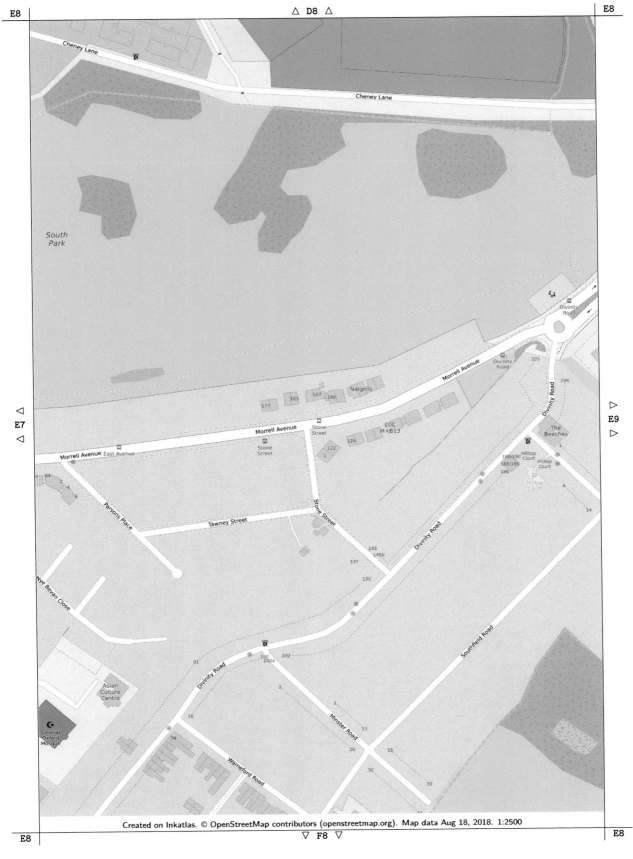

Cheney Lane

Cheney Lane

South Park

Divinity Road

Morrell Avenue

Divinity Road

205

206

Nalgeos

177   183   187   189

Morrell Avenue   Stone Street

20C M+B13

Divinity Road

The Beeches

Morrell Avenue   East Avenue

Stone Street

122   124

1

Hilltop Court

188/190

188/190   Hilltop Court

186   P   Hilltop Court

1

4

84

2   4

6

Parsons Place

Tawney Street

Stone Street

145

146b

137

135

4

14

Nye Bevan Close

Southfield Road

91   Divinity Road

100   102

100a

Asian Culture Centre

2

1

Central Oxford Mosque

76

Minster Road

13

74

30

16

Warneford Road

32

33

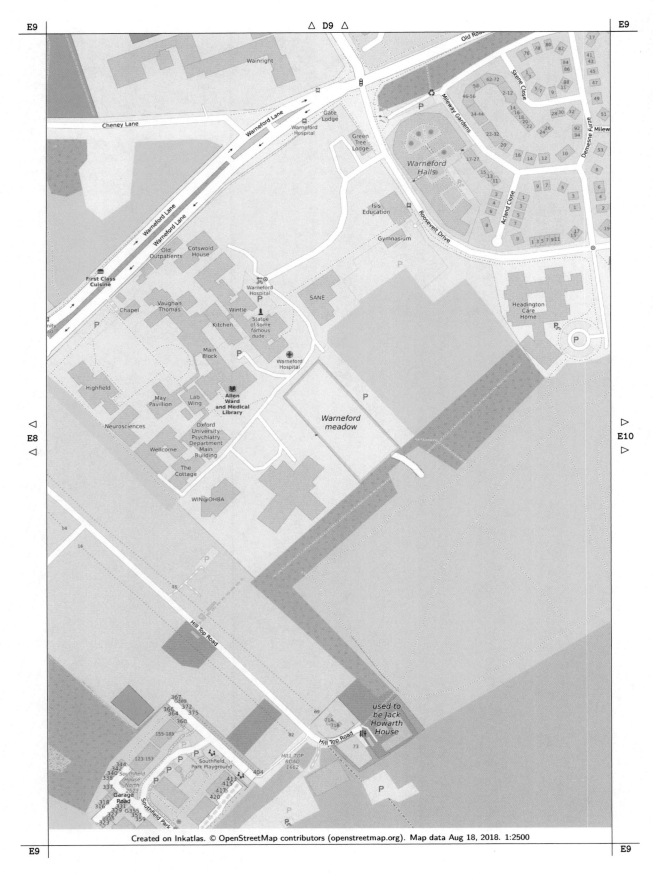

Created on Inkatlas. © OpenStreetMap contributors (openstreetmap.org). Map data Aug 18, 2018. 1:2500

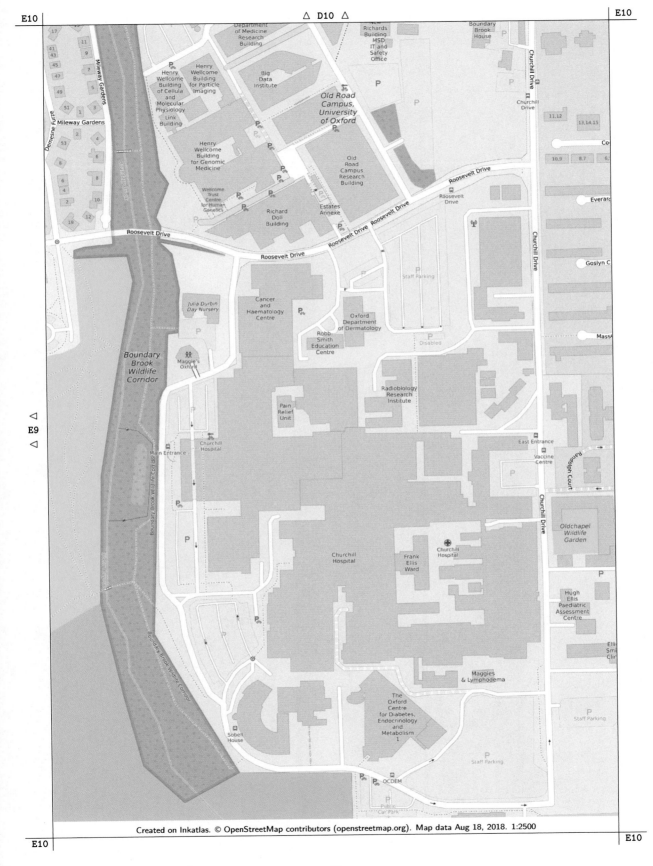

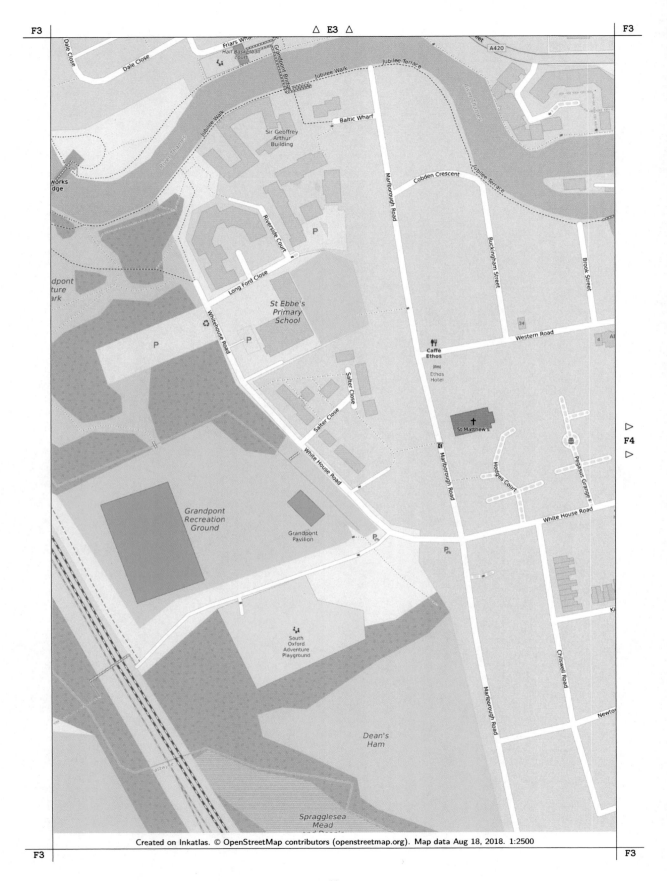

▷
F4
▷

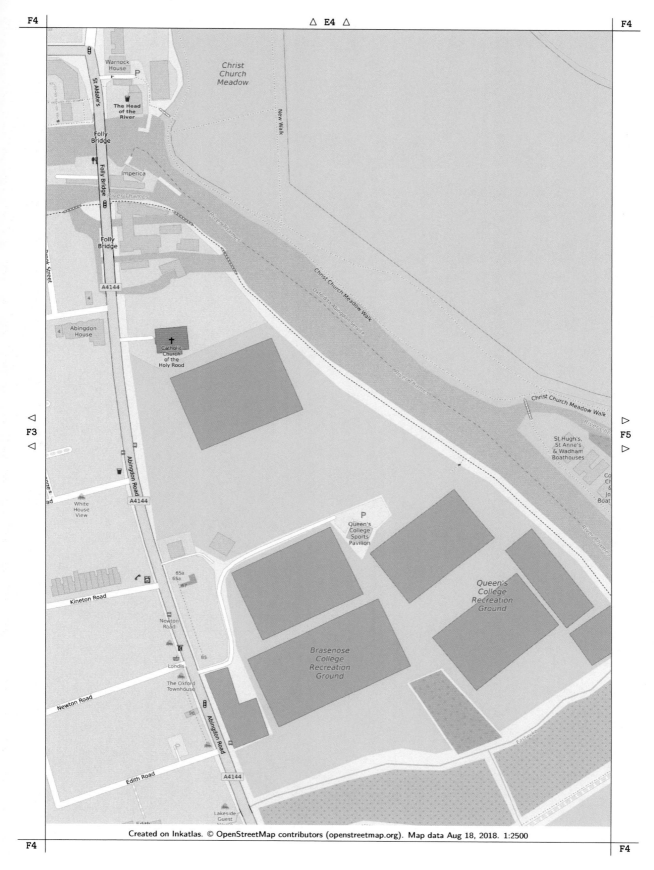

Created on Inkatlas. © OpenStreetMap contributors (openstreetmap.org). Map data Aug 18, 2018. 1:2500

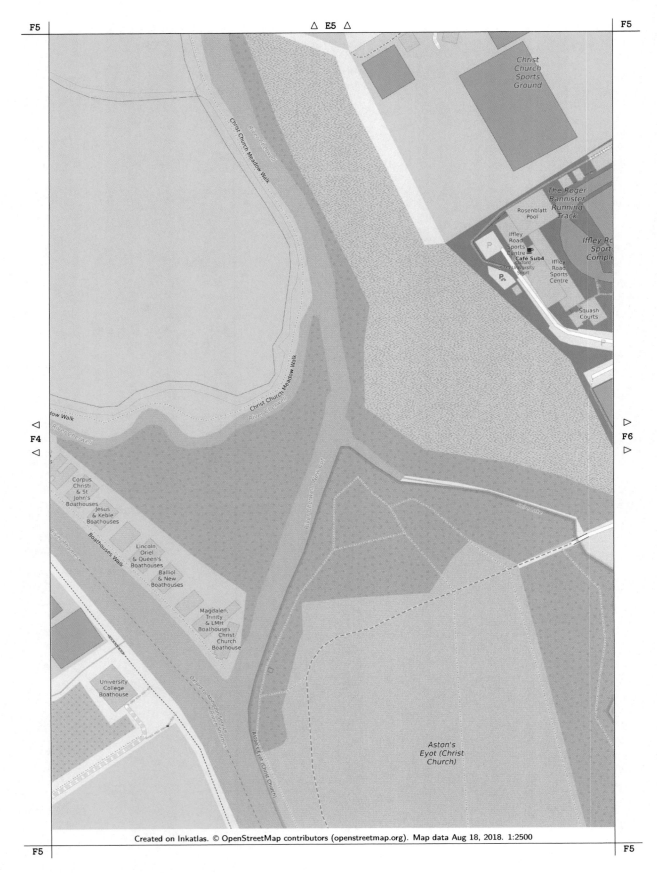

Christ
Church
Sports
Ground

The Roger
Bannister
Running
Track

Rosenblatt
Pool

Iffley
Road
Sports
Centre

Café Sub4
Oxford
University
Sport

Iffley
Road
Sports
Centre

Iffley Rd
Sport
Comple

Squash
Courts

Christ Church Meadow Walk

River Cherwell

Christ Church Meadow Walk

River Cherwell

low Walk

River Cherwell

River Cherwell New Cut

Shireloke

Corpus
Christi
& St
John's
Boathouses

Jesus
& Keble
Boathouses

Lincoln,
Oriel
& Queen's
Boathouses

Balliol
& New
Boathouses

Magdalen,
Trinity
& LMH
Boathouses

Christ
Church
Boathouse

River Thames

Boathouses Walk

University
College
Boathouse

Oxford to Abingdon Service
River Thames

Aston's Eyot (Christ Church)

Aston's
Eyot (Christ
Church)

Created on Inkatlas. © OpenStreetMap contributors (openstreetmap.org). Map data Aug 18, 2018. 1:2500

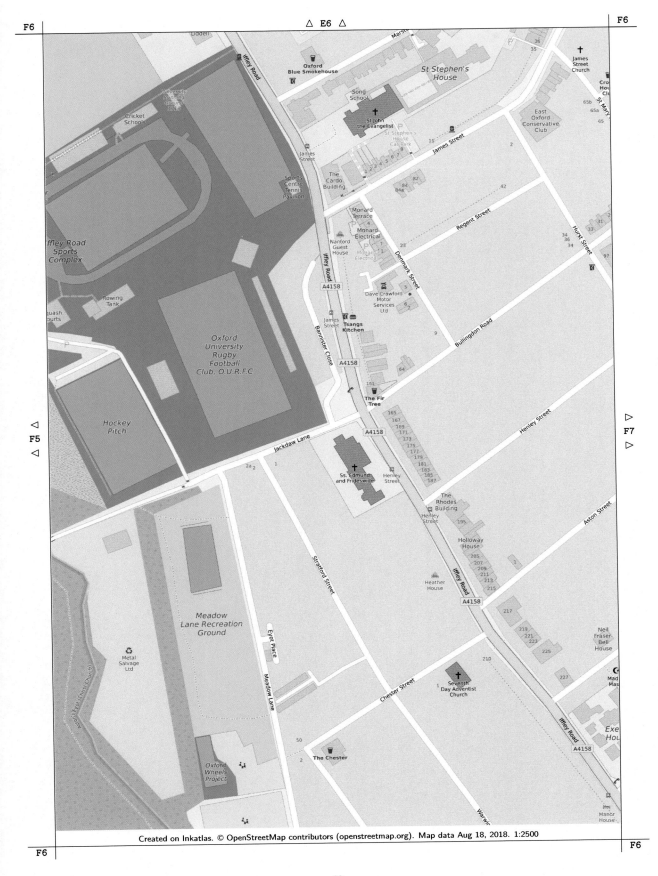

Created on Inkatlas. © OpenStreetMap contributors (openstreetmap.org). Map data Aug 18, 2018. 1:2500

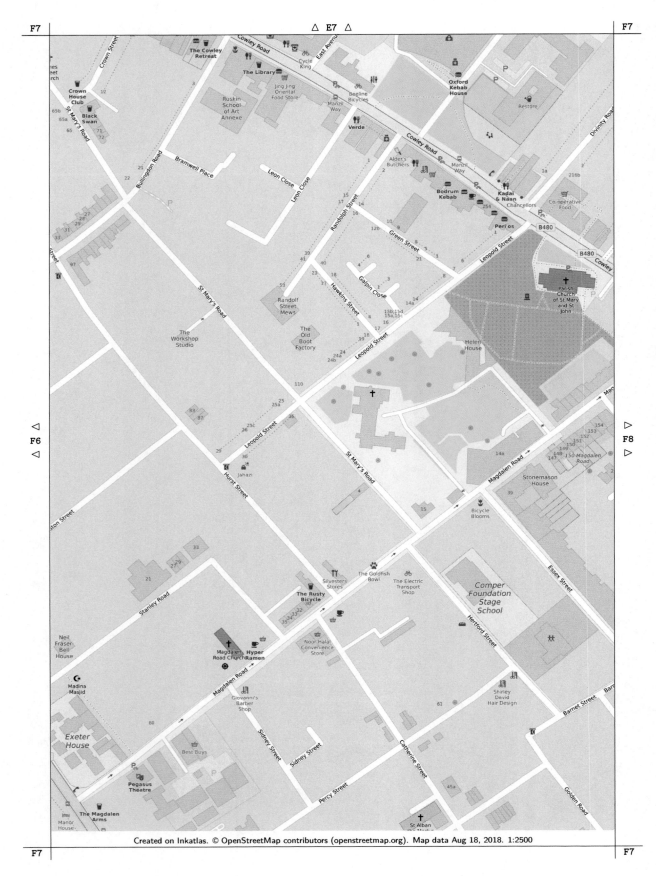

Created on Inkatlas. © OpenStreetMap contributors (openstreetmap.org). Map data Aug 18, 2018. 1:2500

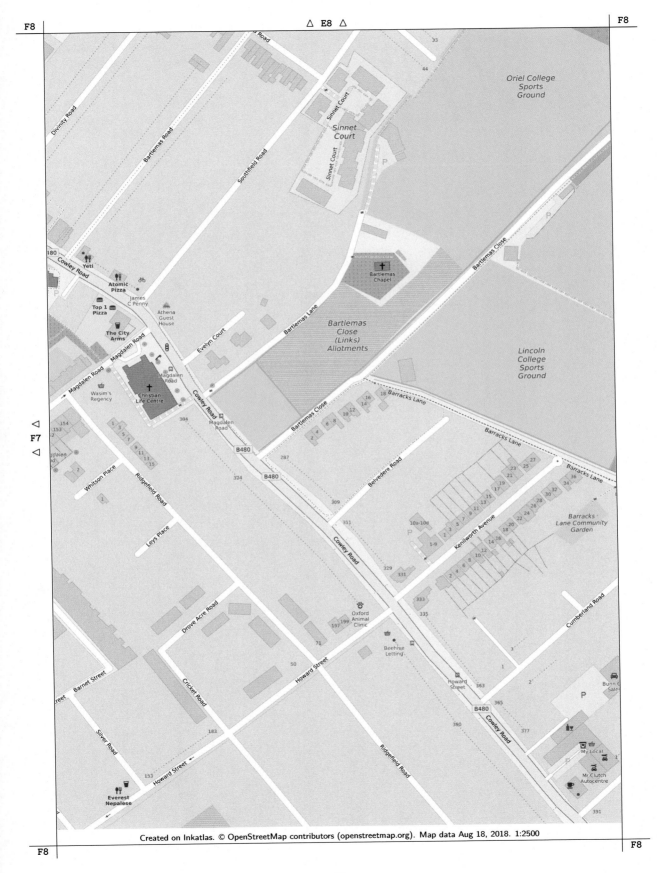

Created on Inkatlas. © OpenStreetMap contributors (openstreetmap.org). Map data Aug 18, 2018. 1:2500

Travel Planner

WHERE?

_____

_____

_____

WHEN?

FROM: ___ / ___ / _____

TO: ___ / ___ / _____

DAYS: _____

TRANSPORTATION

☐ ✈ ☐ 🚌 ☐ 🚗 ☐ ⛴ ☐ 🚲 ☐ 🚶 ☐ _____

DETAILS:

_____

_____

_____

_____

_____

_____

_____

_____

_____

_____

_____

_____

_____

_____

Made in the USA
Coppell, TX
09 May 2021

55347430R00031